BTEC SPORT
ASSESSMENT GUIDE

Unit 4 THE SPORTS PERFORMER IN ACTION

KATHERINE HOWARD

Edited by
Jennifer Stafford-Brown & Simon Rea

The sample learner answers provided in this assessment guide are intended to give guidance on how a learner might approach generating evidence for each assessment criterion. Answers do not necessarily include all of the evidence required to meet each assessment criterion. Assessor comments intend to highlight how sample answers might be improved to help learners meet the requirements of the grading criterion but are provided as a guide only. Sample answers and assessor guidance have not been verified by Edexcel and any information provided in this guide should not replace your own internal verification process.

Any work submitted as evidence for assessment for this unit must be the learner's own. Submitting as evidence, in whole or in part, any material taken from this guide will be regarded as plagiarism. Hodder Education accepts no responsibility for learners plagiarising work from this guide that does or does not meet the assessment criteria.

The sample assignment briefs are provided as a guide to how you might access the evidence required for all or part of the internal assessment of this Unit. They have not been verified or endorsed by Edexcel and should be internally verified through your own Lead Internal Verifier as with any other assignment briefs, and/or checked through the BTEC assignment checking service.

Picture credits

The authors and publishers would like to thank the following for the use of photographs in this volume:

Figure 1.7 © THOMAS DEERINCK, NCMIR/SCIENCE PHOTO LIBRARY; Figure 1.8 © Getty Images/Visuals Unlimited; Figure 1.10 © BSIP, CIOT/SCIENCE PHOTO LIBRARY; Figure of swimmer, page 31 © EpicStockMedia – Fotolia; Figure of boxers, page 31 © olly – Fotolia; Figure of rowers, page 31 © corepics – Fotolia; Figure 2.2 © Rob Bouwman – Fotolia; Figure 2.3 © Mikael Damkier – Fotolia; Figure 2.4 © Stefan Schurr – Fotolia; Figure on page 44 © Maridav – Fotolia; Figure of boxers, page 48 © olly – Fotolia; Figure of tennis player, page 48 © herl – Fotolia.

Every effort has been made to trace and acknowledge ownership of copyright. The publishers will be glad to make suitable arrangements with any copyright holders whom it has not been possible to contact.

Orders: please contact Bookpoint Ltd, 130 Milton Park, Abingdon, Oxon OX14 4SB. Telephone: (44) 01235 827720. Fax: (44) 01235 400454. Lines are open from 9.00–5.00, Monday to Saturday, with a 24 hour message answering service. You can also order through our website www.hoddereducation.co.uk

If you have any comments to make about this, or any of our other titles, please send them to educationenquiries@hodder.co.uk

British Library Cataloguing in Publication Data

A catalogue record for this title is available from the British Library

ISBN: 978 1 444 1 86680

Published 2013

Impression number   10 9 8 7 6 5 4 3 2 1

Year   2016 2015 2014 2013

Copyright © Katherine Howard, Jennifer Stafford-Brown and Simon Rea

All rights reserved. No part of this publication may be reproduced or transmitted in any form or by any means, electronic or mechanical, including photocopy, recording, or any information storage and retrieval system, without permission in writing from the publisher or under licence from the Copyright Licensing Agency Limited. Further details of such licences (for reprographic reproduction) may be obtained from the Copyright Licensing Agency Limited, Saffron House, 6-10 Kirby Street, London EC1N 8TS.

Cover photo © Alex_Mac – Fotolia

Typeset by Integra Software Services Pvt. Ltd., Pondicherry, India

Printed in Dubai for Hodder Education,
an Hachette UK Company,
338 Euston Road,
London NW1 3BH

Contents

Command words — iv
Introduction — 1

Learning aim A: Know about the short-term responses and long-term adaptations of the body systems to exercise — 2
Assessment guidance for learning aim A — 18

Learning aim B: Know about the different energy systems used during sports performance — 38
Assessment guidance for learning aim B — 44

Sample assignment brief: Learning aim A — 56

Sample assignment brief: Learning aim B — 59

Knowledge recap answers — 60

For attention of the learner

You are not allowed to copy any information from this book and use it as your own evidence. That would count as plagiarism, which is taken very seriously and may result in disqualification. If you are in any doubt at all please speak to your teacher.

Command words

You will find the following command words in the assessment criteria for each unit.

Compare and contrast	Identify the main factors relating to two or more items/situations, and explain the similarities and differences, and in some cases say which is best and why.
Describe	Give a clear description that includes all the relevant features. Think of it as 'painting a picture with words'.
Explain	Provide details and give reasons and/or evidence to support the arguments being made. Start by introducing the topic then give the 'how' or 'why'.
Summarise	Demonstrate an understanding of the key facts, and if possible illustrate with relevant examples.

Introduction

Unit 4, The Sports Performer in Action, is an internally assessed, optional, specialist unit with two learning aims:

- Learning aim A: Know about the short-term responses and long-term adaptations of the body systems to exercise
- Learning aim B: Know about the different energy systems used during sports.

The unit focuses on the effects training has on the body, including the short-term effects, such as increased breathing, and the long-term adaptations that occur when someone regularly takes part in sport. Learning aim A looks at the musculoskeletal and cardiorespiratory systems and how they are affected by exercise. In learning aim B you'll cover the energy systems that are used for different kinds of sporting activities, for example, those where a short burst of energy is needed and those where energy is needed for more prolonged activity.

Each learning aim is divided in to two sections. The first section focuses on the content of the learning aim and each of the topics are covered. At the end of each topic there are some knowledge recap questions to test your understanding of the subject. The answers for the knowledge recap questions can be found at the end of the book.

The second section of each learning aim provides support with assessment by using evidence generated by a student, for each grading criterion, with feedback from an assessor. The assessor has highlighted where the evidence is sufficient to satisfy the grading criterion and provided developmental feedback when additional work is required.

At the end of the book are examples of assignment briefs for each learning aim. The sample assignment briefs contain tasks that would allow you to generate the evidence needed to meet all the assessment criteria in the unit.

Learning aim A
Know about the short-term responses and long-term adaptations of the body systems to exercise

Assessment criteria

2A.P1 Describe ways in which the musculoskeletal system responds to short-term exercise.

2A.P2 Describe ways in which the cardiorespiratory system responds to short-term exercise.

2A.P3 Summarise, using relevant examples, long-term adaptations of the musculoskeletal system to exercise.

2A.P4 Summarise, using relevant examples, long-term adaptations of the cardiorespiratory system to exercise.

2A.M1 Explain responses of the musculoskeletal system to short-term exercise.

2A.M2 Explain responses of the cardiorespiratory system to short-term exercise.

2A.M3 Explain long-term adaptations of the musculoskeletal system to exercise.

2A.M4 Explain long-term adaptations of the cardiorespiratory system to exercise.

2A.D1 Using three different sports activities, compare and contrast how the musculoskeletal and cardiorespiratory systems respond and adapt to exercise.

Topic A.1 Short-term effects of exercise on the musculoskeletal system

Increased production of synovial fluid

Studied ☐

A joint is where two or more bones meet. They rub against each other to produce movement.

Synovial joints are a type of joint which share the same characteristics. All synovial joints have the following:

- synovial fluid (Figure 1.1) – to reduce friction and supply nutrients
- cartilage – covering the end of the bones to protect them and prevent rubbing
- ligaments – tough fibres which hold the joints together
- a synovial cavity – this space allows the synovial fluid to be trapped around the joint.

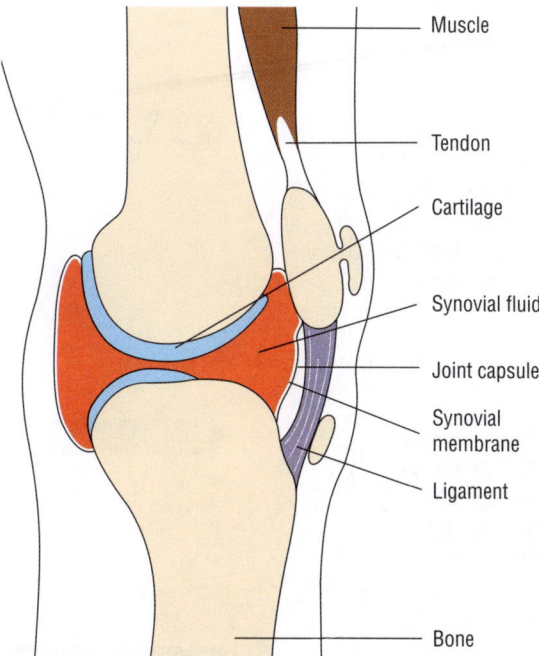

Figure 1.1 A synovial joint

There are six different types of synovial joints:

- ball and socket – e.g. shoulder and hip
- pivot – e.g. atlas and axis in the neck
- hinge – e.g. elbow and knee
- saddle – e.g. thumb
- condyloid – e.g. wrist
- gliding – e.g. small bones in the hands and feet.

Synovial fluid is a lubricant which surrounds the joint, allowing it to move more smoothly. This fluid helps to reduce friction caused by moving the joints. A short-term effect of exercise is that there is an increase in synovial fluid production, which allows the joints to move more freely and provides nourishment for the synovial joints. During exercise, our joints become warmer. This is due to friction being produced as the bones move, which produces some heat which warms the synovial fluid. When the synovial fluid is warmer it can move around the joint more easily. It becomes a better lubricant and helps the joints to move more freely.

Increased joint range of movement

During exercise there is an increase of blood flow to the working muscles and an increase in muscle temperature. This is because heat is produced by the movement of blood through the muscles. The joints warm up when they begin to exercise and the synovial fluid becomes less viscous (thick). This enables the range of movement around our joints to increase.

Micro tears in muscle fibres

When we exercise, we make little tears in our muscles. These micro tears are made in the muscle fibres because we are stretching them further and putting more strain on them. When the micro tears repair, the muscle rebuilds. This process of overloading the muscles allows them to grow slightly bigger and stronger.

Exercise (high-impact activity) encourages new bone formation

During exercise we exert pressure on our bones; this causes them to bend slightly. The repetitive impact of exercising causes the bones to form a new layer. This makes the bones stronger and more able to cope with exercise without fracturing.

Increased metabolic activity

Metabolic activity is the name given to the chemical reactions within our bodies which produce energy. These reactions break down food into smaller molecules, and those reactions which build small molecules into bigger useful blocks speed up.

An effect of short-term exercise is that metabolic activity increases; the chemical reactions take place faster in our bodies.

Knowledge recap

1. What is synovial fluid?
2. Identify two short-term musculoskeletal responses to exercise.
3. What is meant by the term 'metabolic activity'?

Topic A.2 Short-term effects of exercise on the cardiorespiratory system

Increased heart rate

The heart rate increases due to the heart having to work harder to pump oxygenated blood around the body.

The function of the heart is to pump oxygenated (oxygen-rich) blood around the body.

A heartbeat is produced when the heart contracts, and blood is pushed out of the heart. This happens approximately 65 times a minute. Heart rate is recorded as beats per minute (bpm).

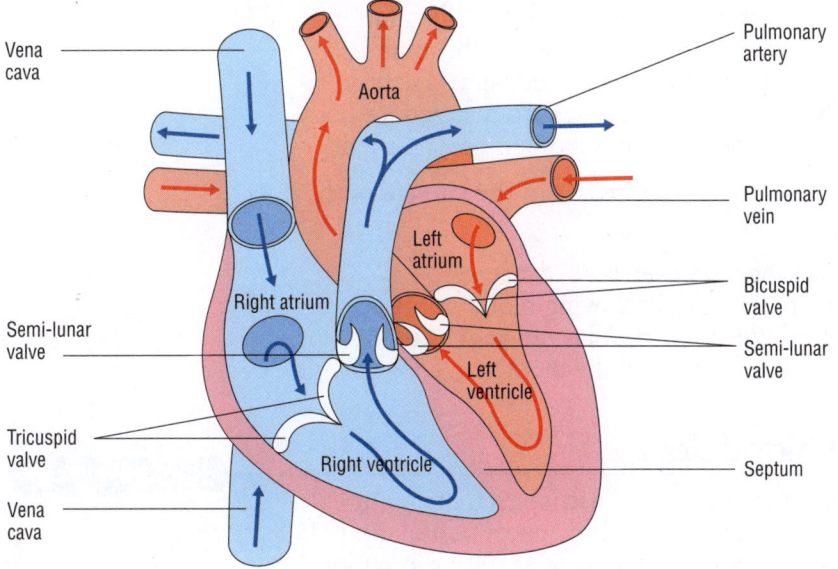

Figure 1.2 The heart

The heart is made of cardiac muscle, a type of involuntary muscle which we cannot control. The heart has four chambers – two atria and two ventricles (Figure 1.2). The heart has a wall in the middle which separates the oxygenated and de-oxygenated blood.

When we exercise, heart rate increases because our body increases the demand for fuel and oxygen. The heart has to work harder and faster to pump oxygenated blood around the body and to the working muscles.

Increased breathing rate

Breathing rate increases in order to supply more oxygen to working muscles and to remove carbon dioxide.

Breathing rate is the number of breaths taken per minute. During exercise, breathing rate increases to allow more oxygen to be taken in to the body and sent to the working muscles. Carbon dioxide, a waste product, is produced during exercise. It needs to be removed from the body because it will cause fatigue.

Increased blood flow

When we exercise, our body needs more oxygen and nutrients. These are delivered by the blood. To get the nutrients around the body faster, our blood flow increases. The nutrients in our blood include glucose, vitamins and minerals which help the body to produce energy.

Sweat production and skin reddening

As we exercise, we create friction. This is because the body/joints are moving faster and the blood inside the body is travelling faster. Friction is caused by rubbing, either bone on bone in the joints or the blood cells pushing through the arteries and veins. Friction creates heat, so our body temperature increases. To help reduce body temperature, our bodies produce sweat and the skin becomes redder.

Sweat is released which is then evaporated from the surface of the skin; this process cools the body.

Our skin becomes redder when we exercise because blood is redirected to the surface of our skin. By moving blood to the skin of our body, heat is brought to the surface and is radiated (lost) into the atmosphere. Our body gives off heat and the blood can cool down.

Redistribution of blood flow

Blood flow is redistributed via the vasoconstriction (narrowing) of arterioles supplying inactive parts of the body, and vasodilation (opening) of arterioles supplying skeletal muscles with more blood and nutrients.

During exercise, the working muscles have an increased demand for blood containing nutrients and oxygen. Blood flow is redistributed to the skeletal or working muscles by the process of **vasoconstriction** and **vasodilation**. By making the arterioles, which carry oxygenated blood from the heart, narrower or more open, blood can be directed to where it is most needed. During vasoconstriction, the walls of the arterioles tighten, making the arteriole narrower. During vasodilation, the walls of the arterioles relax and the arteriole becomes larger and more open.

Figure 1.3 shows the changes to arteriole walls during vasoconstriction and vasodilation.

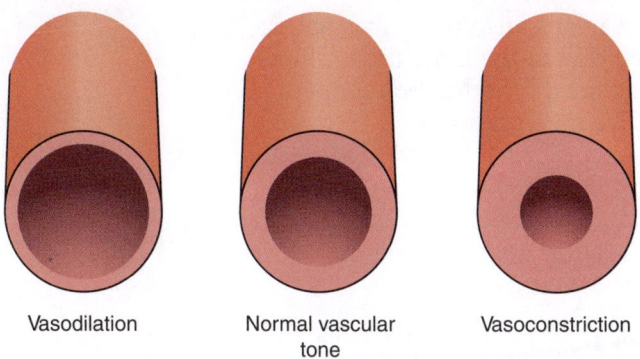

Vasodilation Normal vascular tone Vasoconstriction

Figure 1.3 Vasoconstriction and vasodilation

Increased build-up of lactic acid

Lactic acid is produced when the body creates energy without oxygen. It is a waste product which causes fatigue when it builds up in the muscles. Because the body needs more energy for exercise, more lactic acid is produced. Lactic acid travels around the body in the blood and accumulates in the skeletal muscles, causing the muscle to feel tired.

Increased cardiac output

Cardiac output (Q) is the amount of blood pumped from the left ventricle in one minute. Cardiac output is equal to stroke volume (SV) multiplied by heart rate (HR).

Stroke volume is the amount of blood pumped into the left ventricle in one heart beat/contraction.

Q = SV x HR

The average stroke volume at rest for a healthy 16-year-old male is approximately 70 ml. The average heart rate for a healthy 16-year-old male is approximately 65 bpm. The average cardiac output for a healthy 16-year-old male would therefore be 4550 ml or 4.55 L.

Q = 70 ml x 65 bpm

Q = 4.55 L/min

During exercise, if our 16-year-old male's stroke volume increases to 100 ml and his heart rate increases to 125 bpm, his cardiac output will also increase:

Q = 100 ml x 125 bpm

Q = 12.5 L/min

By increasing the stroke volume and the heart rate, the body is able to pump much more blood around the body in the same time. This increase in cardiac output enables oxygenated blood to be pumped from the heart and to the skeletal muscles much faster.

Increased blood pressure

Blood pressure increases as the cardiovascular system works to deliver more oxygen and glucose to the muscles.

Blood pressure is a measure of the pressure inside the body when the heart contracts and relaxes as it pumps blood around the body. The **systolic** pressure is when the ventricles are contracting and pushing blood out of the heart; the **diastolic** pressure is measured when the ventricles in the heart relax and begin to refill with blood.

When we exercise, blood pressure increases as more oxygen and nutrients are needed in the skeletal muscles. As the systolic pressure increases, the ventricles empty with more force to push the blood out of the heart faster. The diastolic pressure remains unchanged, and the ventricles of the heart will refill at the same speed.

Increased tidal volume

As muscular activity increases, the production of carbon dioxide increases, resulting in an increase in tidal volume.

As we exercise, muscular activity increases and our body produces more carbon dioxide, a waste product of making energy. Carbon dioxide causes the muscles to fatigue and feel tired. It is important that the muscles get rid of carbon dioxide as quickly as possible to prevent fatigue and sports performance decreasing.

Tidal volume (TV) is the amount of air inhaled and exhaled, breathed in and out in one breath. The TV for an average 16-year-old healthy male is 0.5 L. During exercise, TV can increase to 3.0 L. When we exercise, we can exhale larger quantities of carbon dioxide.

Knowledge recap

1. What is heart rate?
2. What is vasoconstriction?
3. What is lactic acid?
4. How does blood pressure alter during exercise?
5. Define tidal volume (TV).

Topic A.3 Long-term adaptations of the musculoskeletal system

Hypertrophy (increased muscle size)

Studied ☐

The definition of hypertrophy is an increase in the size of a tissue or cells.

Muscular hypertrophy happens in the skeletal muscles, and it allows the muscles to grow bigger. To achieve muscular hypertrophy, the skeletal muscles need to be worked harder and for longer periods of time; the result will be larger and stronger muscles.

Hypertrophy is a long-term adaptation to exercise because the muscles are working more frequently, for longer periods of time and at a higher intensity. The muscles have experienced overload, which means that the muscles adapt to cope with a higher workload by growing bigger and stronger.

Increase in bone density

Studied ☐

Calcium is a mineral which is essential for bone growth and development. When we exercise over long periods of time, our bones begin to produce more calcium. This increase in calcium allows the bones to grow stronger and slightly increase in mass, and our bone density actually increases as a long-term adaptation to exercise. This is because our bones have to cope with more impact. When we exercise, our bones absorb the impact; e.g. as we run, the bones in our legs and feet are constantly absorbing the impact of the movement pushing downwards into the ground with every step. An increase in bone strength will allow an athlete's bones to cope better with the impact of long-term exercise.

Figure 1.4 shows how working the skeletal muscles can help bones to become more dense.

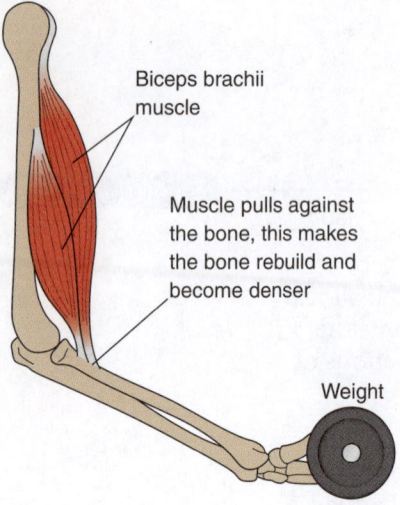

Figure 1.4 How exercise helps increase bone density

Stronger connective tissues

Studied

Connective tissue is a fibrous fibre found throughout the body. Ligaments and tendons are different types of connective tissue (Figure 1.5).

Ligaments are used in the body to connect bones together. They are tough, elastic straps which allow the bones to move at joints.

Tendons are used in the body to attach skeletal muscles to bones. They are tough fibres with very little elasticity. They allow muscles to join to joints and bones to create movements.

A long-term adaptation to exercise is that these connective tissues become stronger. Exercise causes the tissues to become stronger and slightly thicker, which makes them less likely to tear and cause an injury.

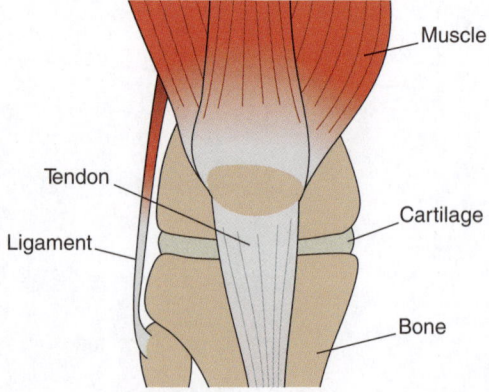

Figure 1.5 Tendons and ligaments

Increased stability of joints

When we exercise, our connective tissue becomes stronger, and the ligaments and tendons improve at holding our joints together. This means that the joints are more stable and we are less likely to get an injury from the tendon or ligament tearing or the joint dislocating. The structures around our joints will become stronger and allow the joints to be more effective at providing a stable range of movement.

Increased thickness of hyaline cartilage

Hyaline cartilage is a type of connective tissue. It is found on the surface of our joints. It has no blood supply and is a very hard and slippery tissue. Hyaline cartilage gets its nutrients from the synovial fluid, which covers it in the joints. It has a very important role. Hyaline cartilage stops the bones rubbing together at joints and also absorbs the impact from exercise.

Figure 1.6 shows hyaline cartilage in a synovial joint.

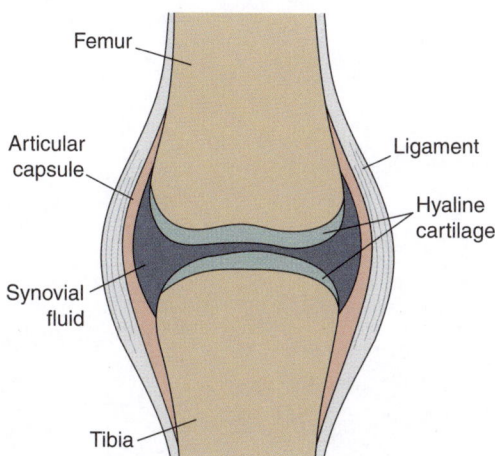

Figure 1.6 A synovial joint

The hyaline cartilage becomes stronger as a long-term adaptation of exercise. This means it can cope with the increasing demands of exercise as the bones rub against each other when swimming or throwing a ball, and it helps to cushion the joints as we land from running and jumping.

Skeletal muscles adapt to using more oxygen

The muscles and their capillaries become more efficient and can therefore work for a longer period of time.

As we exercise for longer, our body adapts to the additional workload. Our skeletal muscles adapt to using more oxygen. This allows our bodies to work for longer periods of time without fatigue setting in. Our muscles become much more efficient at using oxygen so that we can make energy more quickly in our muscle cells. More capillaries surround the skeletal muscles, which can transport oxygen throughout the muscles more quickly. This helps to distribute blood and oxygen to where it is most needed.

Increased number of mitochondria

Mitochondria are very small structures which can be found in muscle cells. Mitochondria produce energy which we use for the skeletal muscles to produce movement. The mitochondria produce adenosine triphosphate (ATP) by using aerobic respiration, with oxygen and glucose. Mitochondria are the energy cells of the body.

Figure 1.7 shows mitochondria in the muscle fibres.

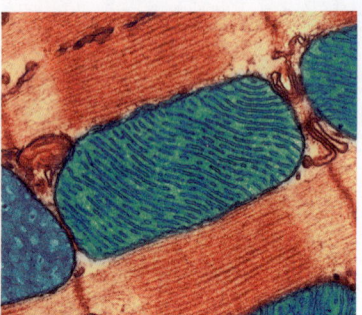

Figure 1.7 The mitochondria in muscle fibres

The size and number of mitochondria can be increased by exercising. This means that an athlete can increase their energy supply to allow them to compete for longer periods of time and at a higher intensity, therefore delaying fatigue.

Decreased risk of osteoporosis

Osteoporosis is an illness which reduces the density of bones. This means that your skeleton becomes very brittle and fragile (Figure 1.8). People who suffer from osteoporosis are likely to experience fractures because their bones have lost calcium and their bone mass has reduced. Osteoporosis is more common in middle-aged and elderly women. Accidents can become very dangerous to people with this illness as the slightest bump can put them at risk of breaking a bone.

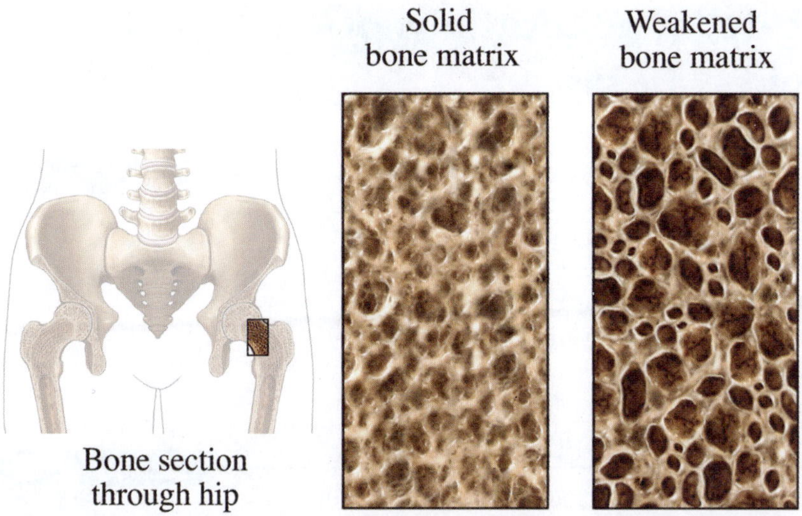

Solid bone matrix   Weakened bone matrix

Bone section through hip

Figure 1.8 How osteoporosis affects bones

By exercising, the risk of osteoporosis can be reduced. The repeated impacts that our bones undergo when we exercise help to strengthen and increase the density of our bones.

Improved posture

Studied ☐

Posture is the position in which you naturally hold your body. Good posture means that all the parts of your body are well aligned. This position puts the least amount of stress on your muscles and joints. Poor posture means that parts of your body are out of alignment. This will put additional stress on your muscles and joints, and may even restrict the space which your organs have inside your body.

A long-term adaptation to exercise is that our skeletal muscles become stronger. The muscles around our core are able to support the weight of our upper body, and this helps to improve our posture. Better posture can help to reduce back and neck pain, and helps the skeleton to become better aligned.

Knowledge recap

1. Give a definition of hypertrophy.
2. What is the difference between ligaments and tendons?
3. What are mitochondria?
4. How can you help to prevent osteoporosis?

Topic A.4 Long-term adaptations of the cardiorespiratory system

Decrease in resting heart rate

As you become fitter, your heart becomes fitter too. This means that your heart has become larger and can pump more blood with every heart beat. Your heart can beat fewer times and still get the same amount of blood around your body. A decreased resting heart rate allows an athlete to take their heart rate up higher when active to benefit their performance.

Increase in heart size and strength

As the heart adapts to exercise, it grows bigger and stronger. The heart is made up of cardiac muscle, a type of involuntary muscle. Just as our skeletal muscles grow bigger with exercise, so does the heart. When muscles increase in size, it is called muscular hypertrophy; when the heart grows bigger, it is called cardiac hypertrophy. A bigger heart has more muscle, and more muscle can produce a larger contraction. A larger heart can push more blood around the body at a higher pressure.

The walls of the left ventricle have become larger; this cardiac muscle has grown bigger and stronger. The left ventricle is the chamber which pushes oxygenated blood out of the heart and around the body. If this chamber is stronger, it can put more force into each contraction and make the blood travel around the body faster.

Increase in stroke volume

Stroke volume increases after prolonged exercise because the heart has grown in size and strength. The left ventricle can now hold more blood, so that every time the heart beats, an increased volume of blood can be pumped out. Remember, stroke volume is the amount of blood leaving the left ventricle in one heart beat or contraction.

Average stroke volume for a male = 50–70 ml

Stroke volume of a trained male athlete = 110–130 ml

The heart can pump more blood per beat, so resting heart rate decreases (bradycardia)

Bradycardia is the technical term for a resting heart rate under 60 bpm. Bradycardia occurs in trained athletes whose hearts have become more efficient and do not need to beat as many times to deliver the body a supply of oxygenated blood. If the heart can pump the same amount of blood around the body with fewer contractions but with more pressure, it is working more effectively.

Decreased risk of hypertension

Hypertension is a chronic condition of high blood pressure. The pressure inside the arteries increases and so the heart has to work harder to pump blood through the blood vessels. Hypertension can be very dangerous and can have life-threatening risks. It can cause heart failure, strokes and kidney disease, and can reduce a person's life span.

A long-term adaptation to exercise is that the heart becomes stronger and more efficient. Exercise increases blood pressure, but this is a good thing as it helps the heart and blood vessels to cope with the extra exertion and this then makes the heart grow bigger and stronger. The benefit of exercise is that it can help to reduce the risk of hypertension and all of the other risks which it can bring.

Increased vital capacity (VC)

Vital capacity (VC) is the maximum amount of air we can breathe out (exhale) after breathing in (inhale) as deeply as we can.

A long-term adaptation to exercise is increased lung volume. Our lungs grow larger and can hold more air. This allows an athlete to inhale and exhale more air. The lungs become more efficient. This means that an athlete can get more oxygen into their body so that they can perform for longer.

Increased efficiency to deliver oxygen and remove waste products

We need oxygen to produce energy. When we perform sports activities, we have a higher demand for energy – the body needs more fuel to be able to sustain the level of activity. To respire aerobically, our muscle cells need oxygen and glucose to make energy. Unfortunately when energy is made in our cells, waste products are created. Carbon dioxide and water are made in the process of producing energy. Water is not too much of a problem; it is not a harmful substance. This can be lost through breathing: when we exhale, water vapour is sent out of our body. Water can also be lost through sweating and urine. Carbon dioxide needs to be removed as soon as possible. When it builds up in our blood, it makes the blood become acidic. The chemical reactions which take place in our body to produce energy need the blood to be neutral. When the blood becomes acidic, reactions will slow down and the production of energy will decrease. As our lungs adapt to exercise and become more efficient, oxygen is delivered and carbon dioxide can be removed more quickly. Carbon dioxide will be taken back to the lungs more effectively so that this gas can be exhaled and removed from our body.

Increased lung efficiency and gaseous exchange

Gaseous exchange occurs in the alveoli or alveolus within the lungs. Oxygen is exchanged in the alveoli for carbon dioxide. This process allows oxygen when inhaled into the lungs to transfer into the capillaries in the lungs, and for carbon dioxide (a waste product) to be transferred into the alveoli to be removed by exhaling. The gases move into the capillaries by diffusion. Diffusion occurs when gases move from a higher concentration to a lower one. For example, when we inhale air there will be a higher concentration of oxygen in the alveoli. The blood in the capillaries surrounding the alveoli has come from the heart and will contain a higher concentration of carbon dioxide. Oxygen will therefore diffuse into the capillaries where there is a lower concentration of this gas, and carbon dioxide will diffuse into the alveoli where there is a lower concentration. This process is known as gaseous exchange.

Figure 1.9 shows the process of gaseous exchange.

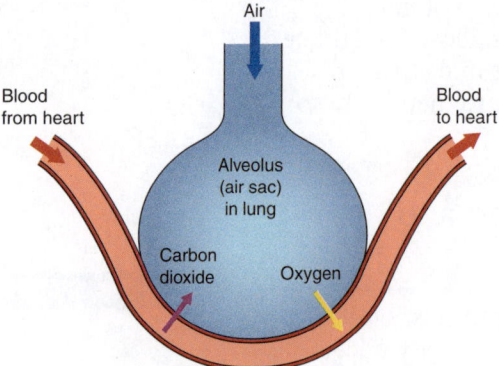

Figure 1.9 The process of gaseous exchange

The lungs adapt to exercise by becoming more efficient. They are able to diffuse oxygen and carbon dioxide more effectively, and gaseous exchange can occur more quickly. The capillary network around the alveoli expands, enabling more gaseous exchange to take place. Increased lung efficiency allows a performer to get oxygen into their body more quickly so that they can work aerobically for longer.

Increased maximum oxygen uptake (VO₂ max)

Studied ☐

Maximum oxygen uptake (or VO_2 max) is the maximum amount of oxygen a person uses in their working muscles while exercising at their maximum capacity. VO_2 max is a very good way to measure a person's endurance performance ability. A higher oxygen uptake will allow the muscles to use oxygen more effectively, and will mean that the athlete can continue working aerobically at a high intensity for longer periods of time. VO_2 max is usually measured in a sports science laboratory using specialised equipment. The equipment can accurately measure the amount of oxygen being used while a person is exercising.

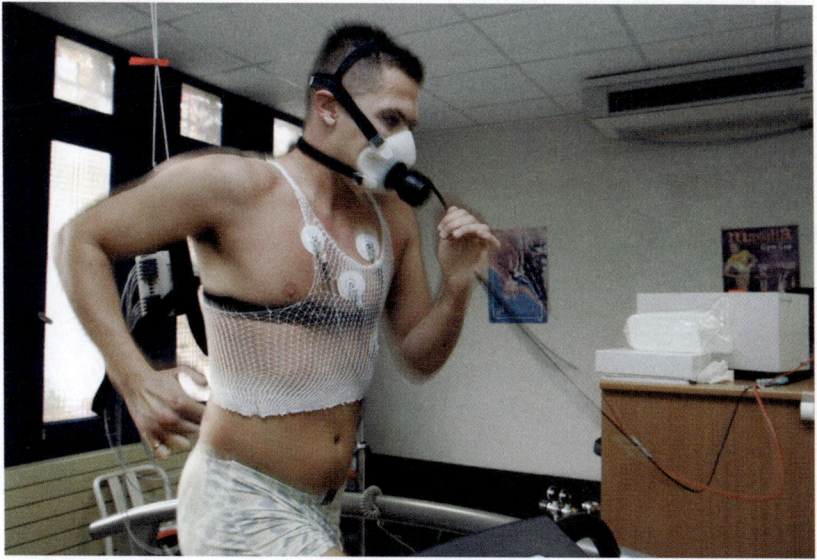

Figure 1.10 An athlete taking a VO_2 max test

Knowledge recap

1. What is meant by the term 'cardiac hypertrophy'?
2. What is an average stroke volume for a male?
3. Why is bradycardia a benefit to a sports person?
4. Name two waste products that the body produces during exercise.

Assessment guidance for learning aim A

Scenario

Your school or college has just had a new gym built next to the sports hall. The gym manager has asked your BTEC Sport group to create an information pack to show how your body responds and adapts to exercise. This information will be displayed in your school gym so that other learners can see the benefits of taking part in exercise.

2A.P1 Describe ways in which the musculoskeletal system responds to short-term exercise

Assessor report: The command verb in the grading criterion is describe. In the learner's answer we would expect to see a detailed account of the ways in which the musculoskeletal system responds to short-term exercise.

Learner answer

The short-term effects of exercise:

1. More synovial fluid is produced.

2. The synovial fluid lubricates the joints.

3. The range of movement at the joints increases. As the body begins to exercise, it moves more and more. The joints warm up and the ligaments surrounding them will stretch a small amount, giving the joints a bigger range of movement. This might mean that a football goal keeper can stretch further and reach the ball to save an attempt on goal.

4. More blood flows to the muscles surrounding the synovial joints. When the body exercises, more blood is sent to the muscles needed to produce movement. An increase in blood flow to the muscles around the moving joints will give them more energy and fuel, and get rid of waste products quicker so that these muscles can work more effectively. A tennis

> player would have more energy going to the muscles around his shoulders and elbows; these muscles will tire more slowly and he will be able to perform better for longer.
> 5. Muscle temperature increases.
> 6. Micro tears occur in the muscle fibres.
> 7. High impact activity allows more bone to be formed.
> 8. Metabolic activity increases.
> 9. More energy is produced.

Assessor report: The learner has identified the ways in which the musculoskeletal system responds to short-term exercise. They have given good descriptions of the responses for 'increased range of movement' and 'more blood to the surrounding muscles'. To achieve 2A.P1 the learner needs to describe in much more detail the other ways in which the body system responds to exercise. The learner should be able to identify and describe at least five short-term responses of the musculoskeletal system to exercise.

Assessor report – overall

What is good about this assessment evidence?

The learner has identified several different musculoskeletal responses to short-term exercise. The learner has put the bullet points in a logical order and has used sports science specific terminology correctly. They have described two of their bullet points with a good level of detail.

What could be improved about this assessment evidence?

Bullet points are very brief; they are a good way of identifying responses but do not allow the learner to provide any description. The learner needs to develop upon their bullet points, to describe in detail the ways the musculoskeletal system responds as they have done for 'increased range of movement' and 'more blood to the surrounding muscles'. The learner needs to show an understanding of this topic, but a list of bullet points does not allow the learner to demonstrate that they can apply their knowledge. Being able to expand at least five of the bullet points would enable the learner to meet the criterion.

2A.P2 Describe ways in which the cardiorespiratory system responds to short-term exercise

Assessor report: The command verb in the grading criterion is describe. In learners' answers we would expect to see a detailed account of the ways in which the cardiorespiratory system responds to short-term exercise.

 Learner answer

The ways the cardiorespiratory system responds to short-term exercise

Response	How	Effect
Increased heart rate	Due to the heart having to work harder to pump oxygenated blood around the body	The heart beats faster as we exercise to get blood around the body
Increased breathing rate	In order to supply more oxygen to working muscles and remove carbon dioxide	The respiratory system makes us breathe more when we exercise to get oxygen into our muscles and carbon dioxide out
Redistribution of blood flow	Via the vasoconstriction (narrowing) of arterioles supplying inactive parts of the body, and vasodilation (opening) of arterioles supplying skeletal muscles with more blood and nutrients	During exercise the blood gets moved around: more goes to the working muscles and less to the other parts of the body
Increased cardiac output	To get oxygenated blood to working muscles (due to increased heart rate and stroke volume)	The heart stretches to get more blood in it and pump the blood around the body to the working muscles when we exercise
Increased blood pressure	As the cardiovascular system works to deliver more oxygen and glucose to the muscles (systolic pressure rises and diastolic pressure remains unchanged)	Blood pressure increases when we exercise so that the body can get more blood to the working muscles faster

Assessor report: The learner has identified some of the ways in which the cardiorespiratory system responds to short-term exercise. To achieve 2A.P2 the learner needs to provide more detailed description of how these systems respond to exercise.

Assessor report – overall

What is good about this assessment evidence?

The learner has identified some of the cardiorespiratory short-term responses to exercise by creating a table. The learner has attempted to describe in their own words what these different responses are. The work is clearly presented in a table format which makes it easy to assess.

What could be improved about this assessment evidence?

The learner has copied and pasted information from the specification and put these statements into their table. This can be useful to the learner as it focuses them on what they need to address. However, work cannot be used for assessment purposes if it has not been written by the learner. Work from other sources must be referenced if it is to be considered for assessment, and must be referred to and used by the learner. The learner needs to develop their own descriptions; they need to give more information about the cardiorespiratory responses to exercise. The learner could use sports examples to help them to describe what is happening in the body of the sports person.

2A.P3 Summarise, using relevant examples, long-term adaptations of the musculoskeletal system to exercise

Assessor report: The command verb in the grading criterion is *summarise*. In their answers we would expect the learner to demonstrate an understanding of key facts relating to long-term adaptations of the musculoskeletal system to exercise, and use relevant examples as part of their answer.

 **Learner answer**

> ### The long-term adaptations of the musculoskeletal system to exercise
>
> The musculoskeletal system is made up of the skeletal muscles, bones and joints. Long-term adaptations to exercise can usually be noticed after six weeks of regular training. These adaptations allow the parts of the body to become more effective at doing their jobs and letting you improve in your sport. Your performance will increase and you will be less likely to have an injury.
>
> The muscle man in my diagram shows the long-term adaptations to exercise on the muscles, bones and joints.

See student diagram opposite.

Assessor report: The learner has identified the long-term adaptations of the musculoskeletal system to exercise, and has summarised, providing relevant examples, the adaptations of lower risk of osteoporosis and increased mitochondria. To achieve 2A.P3 the learner needs to provide similar summaries for the other adaptations.

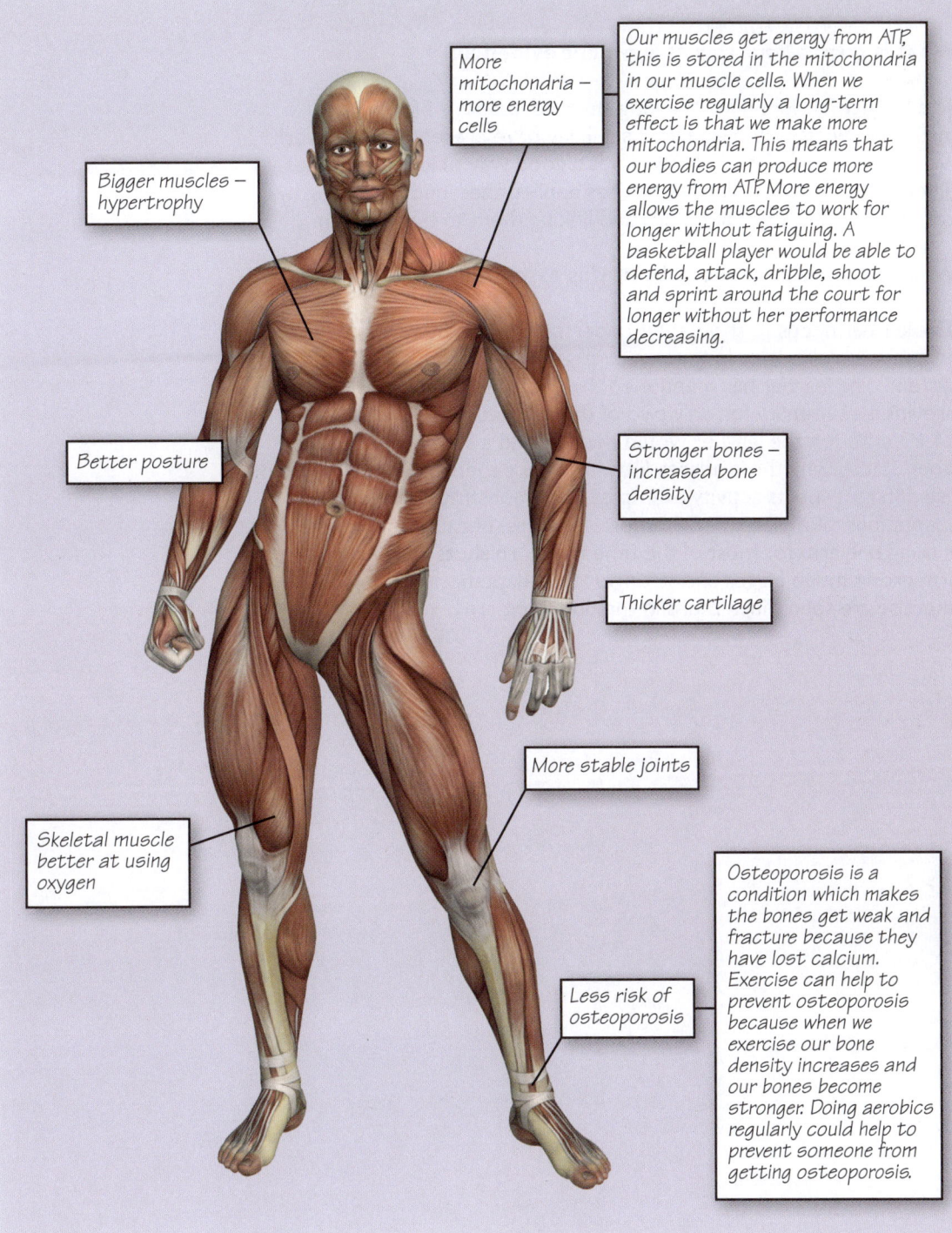

Learning aim A: The short-term responses and long-term adaptations of the body to exercise

Assessor report – overall

What is good about this assessment evidence?

The learner has identified the long-term adaptations of the musculoskeletal system to exercise. They have presented their work well – the use of a labelled diagram is a good way of identifying the different adaptations. The learner has applied their understanding by correctly identifying adaptations and linking them to the diagram.

What could be improved about this assessment evidence?

The learner needs to show their understanding of the main adaptations relating to long-term exercise and the musculoskeletal system. The learner has mentioned the different adaptations but has provided a summary for only two of the adaptations. To achieve the 2A.P3 criterion the learner would need to add a summary to each label, stating why these adaptations have happened. The learner could use different sports activity examples to demonstrate how these adaptations take place. For example, in tennis, because the athlete is using one arm for most of the time to return shots and serve, this arm grows much bigger and stronger; the adaptations to long-term exercise are seen much more in the dominant arm.

2A.P4 Summarise, using relevant examples, long-term adaptations of the cardiorespiratory system to exercise

Assessor report: The command verb in the grading criterion is summarise. In their answers we would expect the learner to demonstrate an understanding of key facts relating to the long-term adaptations of the cardiorespiratory system to exercise, providing relevant examples as part of their answer.

See learner answer opposite.

Assessor report: The learner has briefly summarised the long-term adaptations of the cardiorespiratory system to exercise, providing a longer summary with relevant examples of the adaptation of increased vital capacity. To achieve 2A.P4 the learner needs to provide more relevant examples to supplement their work and include more depth to the rest of their answer.

Assessor report – overall

What is good about this assessment evidence?

The learner has attempted to identify the adaptations with the different structures in the cardiorespiratory system. The learner has identified a few different adaptations and has summarised some of the long-term adaptations (increased vital capacity) to a swimmer.

What could be improved about this assessment evidence?

The learner should expand their work, following the same format. For example, they could identify the adaptations which happen to the lungs and heart, and summarise these together to achieve 2A.P4. The learner should include more sports examples to support their evidence. They could choose one sport and link their examples of the benefits of these long-term adaptations to that sport.

Learner answer

A summary of the long-term adaptations of the cardiorespiratory system to exercise

The cardiorespiratory system comprises the lungs, airways, heart and blood vessels. The diagram below shows the different parts of the cardiorespiratory system.

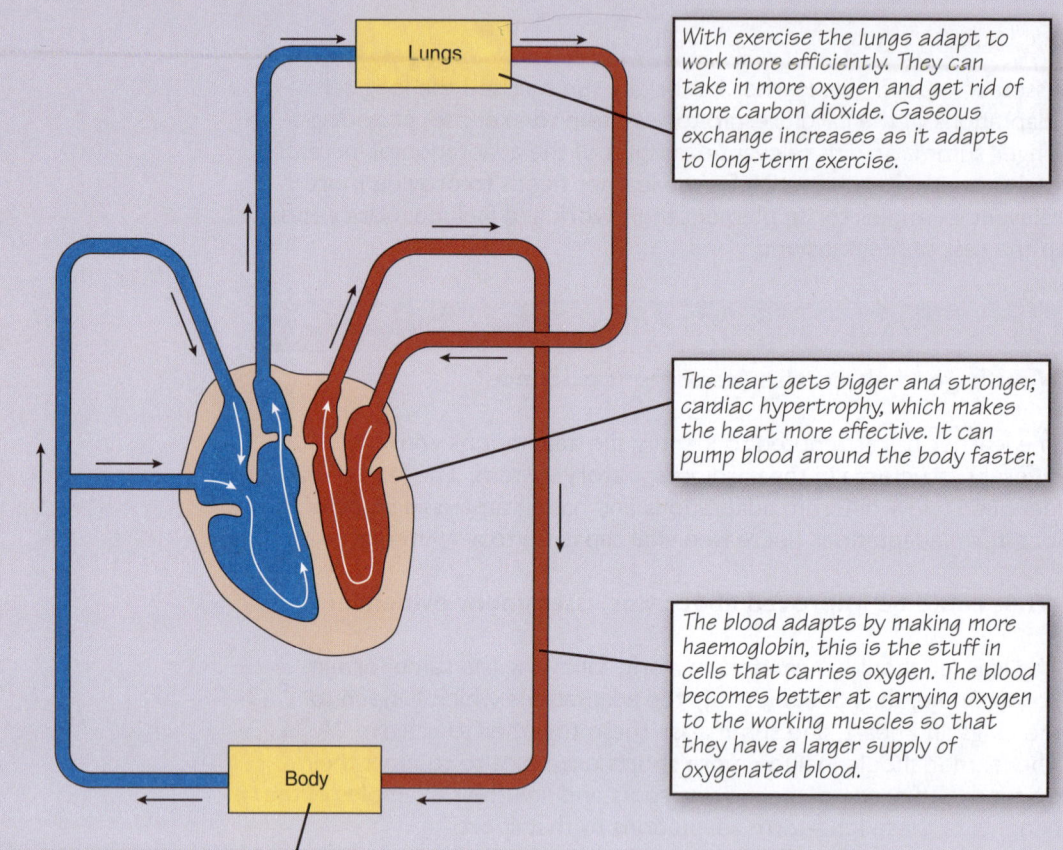

With exercise the lungs adapt to work more efficiently. They can take in more oxygen and get rid of more carbon dioxide. Gaseous exchange increases as it adapts to long-term exercise.

The heart gets bigger and stronger, cardiac hypertrophy, which makes the heart more effective. It can pump blood around the body faster.

The blood adapts by making more haemoglobin, this is the stuff in cells that carries oxygen. The blood becomes better at carrying oxygen to the working muscles so that they have a larger supply of oxygenated blood.

Muscle tissue has a better supply of oxygenated blood and a more efficient system for removing carbon dioxide. The long-term adaptations of the cardiorespiratory system allow the muscles to work for longer.

For example, a swimmer benefits from having an increased vital capacity because they can get more air into their lungs, which means they are able to diffuse more oxygen into their blood which can be transported to the muscles to provide them with a larger supply of oxygen. More oxygen enables a swimmer to work aerobically for longer. The swimmer may be able to swim longer distances or at a higher intensity, increasing their performance.

2A.M1 Explain responses of the musculoskeletal system to short-term exercise

Assessor report: The command verb in the grading criterion is *explain*. In their answers we would expect to see that the learner had developed the points made for 2A.P1 and provided more depth about how the musculoskeletal system responds to short-term exercise.

 Learner answer

Responses of the musculoskeletal system to short-term exercise

During exercise, the musculoskeletal system produces more synovial fluid. This fluid acts as a lubricant, allowing the joint to move more freely and smoothly. When we exercise, our bodies create friction in our joints. This produces heat in the joints as they move; this heat helps the synovial fluid to become thinner. The warm fluid can move around the joint more easily, which increases the range of movement we can experience at our joints. For example, a cricketer will be able to move their shoulder through a larger range of movement, and this will help them to produce a better bowling action to be able to bowl their opponent out.

During exercise, blood is redirected to the working muscles, the muscles surrounding the joints we are using. For example, the major joints used during rowing are those in the knees and elbows. More blood will go to the muscles around these joints, providing the muscles with energy and oxygen.

Assessor report: The learner has provided a sound explanation of the effect of short-term exercise on joints. However, there is a lot of evidence missing; the learner has not completed this task. To achieve 2A.M1 the learner would need to explain the short-term effects of exercise on the other areas of the musculoskeletal system, e.g. the muscles, bones and metabolic activity.

Assessor report – overall

What is good about this assessment evidence?

The learner has provided a relevant example to help explain how the short-term effect on the joints can increase performance in a cricket player.

What could be improved about this assessment evidence?

The learner could include diagrams to help explain their evidence. The learner could develop their bullet points from P1 as they have begun to in this M1 task, and ensure that they address all of the bullet points with more depth.

2A.M2 Explain responses of the cardiorespiratory system to short-term exercise

Assessor report: The command verb in the grading criterion is explain. In their answers we would expect to see that the learner had developed the points made for 2A.P2 and provided more depth about how the cardiorespiratory system responds to short-term exercise.

Learner answer

The cardiorespiratory system responses to short-term exercise:

Short-term response	Explanation with hockey examples
Increased heart rate	When we begin a warm-up in hockey, our heart starts to work faster and our heart rate increases. The heart pumps blood around the body. Blood contains nutrients and oxygen which are both essential for exercise. The heart rate increases to meet the working muscles' increased demand for nutrients and oxygen during exercise.
Increased breathing rate	During a game of hockey you will notice your breathing rate increase; you will be breathing more often and more deeply. This allows the lungs to take in more oxygen which can be delivered to the working muscles, and also allows more carbon dioxide to be breathed out. If our muscles keep carbon dioxide in them, they will become tired and stop working so well.
Increased cardiac output	Throughout the duration of a hockey match, the working muscles need much more oxygen and nutrients. The body meets this demand by increasing the heart rate and stroke volume; this means that the amount of blood being pumped out of the heart every minute increases to get oxygenated blood to working muscles.
Increased blood pressure	When playing hockey, our blood pressure increases so that the cardiovascular system (the heart and blood vessels) can provide more oxygen and nutrients to the working muscles. Blood pressure measures the force of our blood as it leaves the heart. The systolic pressure is when the blood is pushed out of the ventricles as the heart contracts; the pressure increases during exercise. The diastolic pressure is created as the ventricles relax and begin to refill with blood; this pressure remains unchanged while we are active.

Assessor report: The learner has explained some of the cardiorespiratory system responses to short-term exercise. To achieve 2A.M2 the learner needs to address more responses.

Assessor report – overall

What is good about this assessment evidence?

The learner has explained some of the main cardiorespiratory system responses to short-term exercise. They have linked their answers to a sport, using hockey examples. This has enabled the learner to show a good level of understanding about this topic and they have shown that they can apply their knowledge correctly to a sports situation. The work has been set out in a table format which has allowed the learner to expand on each response in their own words.

What could be improved about this assessment evidence?

The learner has not provided enough different responses to exercise. They should aim to include the majority of the cardiorespiratory system responses to short-term exercise. At present there has not been enough work produced for the learner to achieve the 2A.M2 criterion. The learner has not included many technical terms or units. To improve this piece of work, it would be good to see the learner using the correct terms and units of measurement throughout their work. For example, when referring to cardiac output the learner could explain what this is (give a definition), explain how it is measured and describe its unit of measurement. To develop the work further, the learner could try to explain the relationship between the responses, which would show a very good level of understanding of the topic. For example, the learner could explain how cardiac output (Q) is linked to heart rate (HR) and stroke volume (SV), and what happens to Q when HR and SV increase.

2A.M3 Explain long-term adaptations of the musculoskeletal system to exercise

Assessor report: The command verb in the grading criterion is explain. In their answers we would expect to see that the learner had developed the points made for 2A.P3 and provided more depth about the long-term adaptations of the musculoskeletal system to exercise.

Learner answer

I am going to explain how different sports activities can help the musculoskeletal system adapt to exercise to enhance the performance of the sports person.

As you can see in the picture above, swimming uses all of the body's joints. A long-term adaptation to swimming will be better posture. Swimming helps to develop the major muscles in the arms, legs and core. With these muscles being bigger and stronger, the swimmer will achieve an **improved posture**. Stronger muscles help the body to align better; this means that the body is in its natural position, not stooped over. The muscles and joints will experience less stress and pain, and all movements the athlete makes from this good posture position will be better for the body. This will make the athlete less prone to injury.

Boxers train very hard for hours every day to reach the right level of fitness for their fight. Boxers will do lots of strength training to increase the size and strength of their muscles. **Hypertrophy** of the skeletal muscles means that the boxer can fight for longer without his muscles tiring, and he can get more power behind his punches. Because the boxer trains so much, his muscles overload: they adapt to cope with the increased amount of exercise by growing in size and strength.

Rowing is a very demanding sport. It requires a lot of strength, stamina and muscular endurance. The races demand a very high pace and are over long

distances, so rowers need a lot of energy to get them through the race in a winning position. A useful long-term adaptation to a rower would be an **increased number of mitochondria**. Mitochondria are like the body's batteries. They store energy which can then be released whenever it is needed. Mitochondria are very small cell-like structures inside muscle tissue cells. They contain ATP which is the body's source of fuel. If long-term exercise causes the body to produce more energy, the rower will have more fuel to power him on for longer and he will be more successful and less tired.

Assessor report: The learner has explained three of the long-term adaptations of the musculoskeletal system to exercise. They have used photographs and sports examples to demonstrate their knowledge and understanding of this topic. To achieve 2A.M3 the learner needs to provide more information; most of the adaptations should be covered to achieve this criterion.

Assessor report – overall

What is good about this assessment evidence?

The learner has explained three of the adaptations. They have included photographs to show which sports these adaptations can be relevant to, and have given a sports example to develop their explanations. The learner has shown a good deal of understanding; by using a sports example they have applied their knowledge in a specific sports situation.

What could be improved about this assessment evidence?

The learner has made a very good start, but there are too many adaptations missing for this work to be awarded with the 2A.M3 criterion. If the learner completed all of the adaptations in this way, with a photo and a sports-specific example, they would be able to meet the criterion fully.

2A.M4 Explain long-term adaptations of the cardiorespiratory system to exercise

Assessor report: The command verb in the grading criterion is explain. In their answers we would expect to see that the learner had developed the points made for 2A.P4 and provided more depth about long-term adaptations of the cardiorespiratory system to exercise.

Learner answer

The long-term adaptations of the cardiorespiratory system to exercise

A decreased resting heart rate allows an increased amount of oxygen to be circulated around the body without having to increase the heart rate. Sportsmen and women can enhance their performance as the heart is able to accommodate higher oxygen demands that strenuous cardiac exercise and activities demand, and thus increase fitness levels. For example, when playing five-a-side football (which is extremely stop-start with bursts of energetic running), a player will have an advantage if he can raise and rest his heart rate with quicker recovery times, allowing him to play for longer and stave off fatigue.

The heart increases in size and strength. Sportsmen and women can work harder but experience a lower heart rate, which incurs less perceived fatigue. For example, a footballer can run for long times and keep going at a higher intensity for the duration of a football match, without tiring too quickly.

An increase in stroke volume means that a higher rate of oxygen is passed around the body, thus satisfying the energy and muscular needs which allows the body to perform at a higher rate of exercise or physical exertion. For example, a swimmer will be able to swim faster than other competitors and win the race.

The heart will be able to push more blood out of the ventricles with each contraction, so that the resting heart rate can decrease. This means that the body can receive oxygenated blood more effectively. For example, a long-distance/marathon runner would be able to pace themselves better and ensure energy reserves to complete the race in quicker time.

Assessor report: The learner has explained the main long-term adaptations of the cardiorespiratory system to exercise. To achieve 2A.M4 the learner needs to explain further adaptations.

Assessor report – overall

What is good about this assessment evidence?

The learner has explained some of the cardiorespiratory long-term responses to exercise by producing written prose. The learner has explained the different adaptations in their own words, and has given a relevant sports example for each one. The learner has shown a good level of understanding and has chosen sports examples which correctly highlight the named adaptation.

What could be improved about this assessment evidence?

The learner has made a good start to their piece of work. To achieve 2A.M4 they need to address more adaptations. At present there is not enough evidence to be able to award the criterion. The learner could explain the adaptations together and then develop their work by describing how these adaptations can benefit sports performers.

2A.D1 Using three different sports activities, compare and contrast how the musculoskeletal and cardiorespiratory systems respond and adapt to exercise

Scenario

Your school or college has just had a new gym built next to the sports hall. The gym manager has asked your BTEC Sport group to create three posters which compare and contrast how the musculoskeletal and cardiorespiratory systems respond and adapt to exercise. Each poster should show a different sports activity. These posters will be displayed in your school gym so that other learners can see the benefits of taking part in exercise.

Assessor report: The command verbs in the grading criterion are **compare** and **contrast**. In their answers we would expect to see learners identify the main factors in three situations, then explain the similarities and differences in how the musculoskeletal and cardiorespiratory systems respond and adapt to exercise.

Learner answer

I have created three posters which compare and contrast how the musculoskeletal and cardiorespiratory systems respond and adapt to exercise. I have focused each poster on a different sport. Poster one looks at the body's adaptations during swimming, poster two shows football and poster three is about rugby.

SWIMMING
How the body systems respond and adapt to swimming

Musculoskeletal system	Cardiorespiratory system
Similarities	
Increased blood flow: During swimming, both of these systems are working harder. This means that blood needs to get through the systems faster, to deliver nutrients and take away waste products.	
Increased temperature: When we move our bodies, we generate heat. Even in the swimming pool where the water may be slightly cool, we still produce heat. Because both of these systems are working harder, heat is generated because of friction. Friction produces heat in our bodies as the blood rushes through the veins and arteries.	
Increased joint range of movement and muscular activity: Both systems move more during swimming. As we make the movements needed for swimming, we increase the range of movement at the joints being used: knee, hip, shoulder, elbow and neck. As we breathe deeper and faster when we swim, our cardiorespiratory muscles move more and so there is an increase in muscular activity.	
Differences	
Increased production of synovial fluid	Increased heart rate
Micro tears in muscle fibres	Increased breathing rate
These responses to swimming are different because they are specific to the body systems. They are all responses which increase something. As the body is working harder during swimming, the systems increase their responses so that the body can cope with the exercise, and the responses are all inter-related. For example, heart rate increases, which allows the blood to move around the body more quickly, and this increases blood pressure. Breathing rate increases, which gets oxygen into the body more quickly and can then be delivered to the working muscles.	

● ● ● ● ● ● ● ● The benefits to the swimmer ● ● ● ● ● ● ● ●

Increased strength at the joints will enable the swimmer to move faster and for longer. This will allow them to perform strokes more skillfully and precisely, and help them to keep going for longer at a faster speed.

Increased flexibility allows the swimmer to perform techniques more effectively, so they swim better and faster. The swimmer will move through the water more aerodynamically and therefore faster.

Increased temperature means that the swimmer's metabolic reactions are working faster. This enables energy to be released more quickly, which allows the muscles to work more effectively and therefore perform better and faster.

Micro tears in the muscles will repair and grow bigger and stronger because the swimmer is adapting to exercise. This means that they will be able to grow bigger muscles which will produce more power and speed.

The swimmer will have increased speed, strength and stamina. Their body will become fitter and work more effectively. They will have a lower risk of injury and their body will be able to recover more quickly from injuries that do occur. The result of these adaptations is that the swimmer will improve their performance, helping them to do better in training, learn skills correctly and to achieve more in competitions.

Assessor report: The learner has said that they have produced three different sports posters, but they have included only one here. The poster has enabled the learner to compare and contrast how the musculoskeletal and cardiorespiratory systems respond and adapt to exercise. To achieve 2A.D1 the learner would need to include all three posters for assessment. The learner has included only short-term responses to exercise. To achieve the criterion, the learner will need to include short-term and long-term responses and adaptations to exercise.

Assessor report – overall

What is good about this assessment evidence?

The learner has identified several different musculoskeletal and cardiorespiratory responses to short-term exercise. The learner has presented their work in a straightforward way and has annotated their comments as much as possible in a poster format. The learner has linked all of their work to a swimmer and to the benefits of swimming on the musculoskeletal and cardiorespiratory systems. The use of photos has made the poster look appealing; this will make it more likely to be used by the learners in the school or college gym. The learner has developed their answer well to show exactly how a swimmer's body responds to short-term exercise and how this may benefit performance.

What could be improved about this assessment evidence?

It can be difficult to include the content required to achieve a distinction in a poster format. A good way to ensure that this is done could be to add textboxes to the poster and use sub-headings to identify where each statement is being made. To ensure that the learner shows an understanding of this topic, they must develop all of their responses to show that they know what is happening to the body systems as a result of exercise. Because they have included only one of the three posters, it is impossible to know whether the learner would have gone on to include more detail. The learner must also ensure that they include short- and long-term responses and adaptations to exercise. The learner has chosen sports which have similar demands on the body. To extend, it would be beneficial to select sports with different demands on the body, such as gymnastics, canoeing and football. By selecting different types of sports, the learner will allow themselves more scope to apply their knowledge.

Learning aim B
Know about the different energy systems used during sports performance

Assessment criteria

2B.P5 Describe the function of the three energy systems in the production and release of energy for sports performance.

2B.M5 Using two selected sports, explain how the body uses both the anaerobic and aerobic energy systems.

2B.D2 Compare and contrast how the energy systems are used in sports with different demands.

Topic B.1 The anaerobic energy system – not using oxygen

The anaerobic energy system creates energy without using oxygen. This type of energy can be produced for only a very short period of time, but allows the sports person to work at a high intensity. Sports activities which use this energy system last for only a few seconds, such as throwing a punch in boxing, performing a golf swing or taking a penalty kick.

Topic B.2 ATP-CP/alactic acid anaerobic system

Reliance on stored ATP

Adenosine triphosphate (ATP) is a molecule that produces energy in the cells of all living things. In sport we rely on the ATP which is stored in the mitochondria in our muscle cells.

ATP is made up of an adenosine molecule with three phosphates. Energy is released when the bonds between the adenosine and the phosphates break. This energy supply lasts up to four seconds. The energy produced powers high intensity, short duration sports activities. Activities fuelled by this energy system may be used for a discuss throw, a long jump or performing a lay-up in basketball.

Creatine phosphate (CP) helps restore ATP

Creatine phosphate (CP) is made up of a creatine molecule and a phosphate.

CP is stored in the muscle cells and is used to help restore ATP molecules without using oxygen, so that they can be used again to produce energy. CP releases energy when the bond between the creatine and phosphate breaks.

CP is restored aerobically (with oxygen)

CP can be restored in order to release energy again, but this requires oxygen.

In the recovery phase after exercising, oxygen is used to restore the bond between the creatine and phosphate.

Energy is supplied by ATP and CP (four to twenty seconds)

The energy released by ATP and CP will last for between four and twenty seconds. This may be the energy needed for a sprinter to complete a 100 m race, or for a footballer to intercept a pass and dribble on to score a goal. The energy made by ATP and CP will produce high intensity and low duration activities. After 20 seconds, the body's creatine supply will be exhausted. The body can store only a small amount of CP, so that once the bonds have been broken and the energy has been released, CP will no longer produce energy.

When this system runs out of ATP-CP stores, glycolysis takes place

When the ATP and CP stores have been used up, glycolysis will take over. Glycolysis is the breakdown of glucose to produce energy. This is an anaerobic energy system because it works without the need for oxygen. This means that the performer has a constant supply of energy, so can continue to perform.

Knowledge recap

1. What is meant by anaerobic?
2. Name two sports activities which use the anaerobic energy system.
3. What is ATP?
4. How long does ATP-CP energy last?
5. What is glycolysis?

Topic B.3 Glycolysis/lactic acid anaerobic system

ATP is made from glucose stored in the liver and muscles

Glycolysis or lactic acid anaerobic system produces energy quite quickly by using glucose and not using oxygen. Glucose is the sugar our bodies need to make energy. We can get glucose into our blood and delivered to our muscles quite quickly by eating a very sugary food, such as a chocolate bar. We cannot keep much glucose in our blood, so it is stored in the liver and the muscles. This means that we have a store of energy to call on whenever we need it. Glucose is stored as a slightly different substance called glycogen. Our body turns glucose into glycogen to store it, so it can be ready when needed.

Figure 2.1 shows how glucose is stored as glycogen in our muscles and converted into energy by glycolysis when needed.

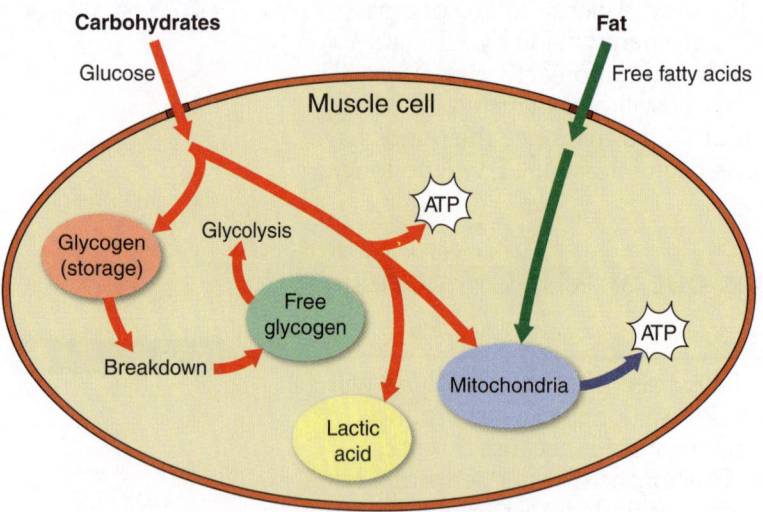

Figure 2.1 How glucose is stored and converted to energy

Energy is supplied by ATP, CP and muscle glycogen (20 to 45 seconds)

The energy produced by ATP, CP and muscle glycogen will give 20–45 seconds of high intensity energy. After 45 seconds, these systems begin to run out and produce energy less effectively. This energy would give the performer fuel to perform a 200 m sprint or 50 m swim.

Energy is supplied by muscle glycogen (45 to 240 seconds)

The energy produced by glycolysis or the lactic acid anaerobic system provides enough energy for a performer to work at a high intensity for 45–240 seconds. The glucose stored in our muscle cells as glycogen is used by the glycolysis energy system without oxygen to produce enough energy for a boxer to fight a three minute round, or for a cricketer to bat and score four runs.

Waste product is lactic acid

Lactic acid is a waste product produced when glucose is used to make energy without oxygen.

Because glucose is being used without oxygen, it cannot be fully broken down into water and carbon dioxide. Instead it is partially broken down into lactic acid. Once oxygen is used to break down the lactic acid, it is converted into water and carbon dioxide, and safely removed from the muscles. Lactic acid can be a problem when it starts to build up in the muscles. A build-up of lactic acid can cause muscles to fatigue, which leads to a rapid decrease in performance. It is very important for sports people to remove lactic acid from their muscles as soon as possible.

When this system is unable to maintain energy requirements, the aerobic system starts to produce energy

Because glucose is being broken down to produce energy without oxygen, lactic acid is produced as a waste product. Lactic acid makes the acidity of the blood increase. When the blood becomes acid, chemical reactions which take place at a lower acid level stop working. The lactic acid (waste product) is actually causing the lactic acid system to stop working. Once this happens, the aerobic system starts to take over. This uses oxygen to make energy from glucose, and this energy system can use lactic acid to make energy and harmless waste products.

Sports that use this system to provide energy are moderate to high intensity

Activities which use this energy system are at a moderate to high intensity level and for a short duration. Activities can include running middle distances, swimming short distances and set sequences in games, e.g. taking a short corner in hockey.

Knowledge recap

1. What is glycogen?
2. What is lactic acid?
3. Why is it important to get rid of waste products?

Topic B.4 The aerobic energy system – using oxygen

During longer periods of exercise/activity, sustained energy relies on this system

Sports that mainly use this system to provide energy for sustained activity are long-distance events such as marathon running, long-distance swimming or long-distance cycling.

The aerobic energy system uses oxygen to convert glucose or fatty acids into energy. Activities which last for over 240 seconds use this energy system. Activities such as long-distance events, marathons, triathlons, open water swimming and long-distance cycling will use this energy system to provide fuel.

Figure 2.2

Energy supplied by muscle glycogen and fatty acids (240 to 600 seconds)

The aerobic energy system produces energy after the ATP-CP system and glycolysis or anaerobic lactic acid system have finished working. This system can produce energy for up to 600 seconds. As long as there is oxygen and glucose (glycogen) or fatty acids, the system can keep producing energy. See Figure 2.3.

Uses oxygen as a means of making energy (re-synthesising ATP)

The aerobic energy system uses oxygen to re-synthesise ATP. This means that when ATP releases energy, the bonds between the adenosine and the phosphates break. In order to re-use the ATP, the bonds need to be restored. The aerobic energy system uses oxygen and glucose or fatty acids to re-synthesise these bonds so that the ATP can be used again and again, and energy can continually be released. See Figure 2.4.

Figure 2.3

Figure 2.4

Low to moderate intensity (beyond 90 seconds)

The aerobic energy system produces energy which will support a sports performer at a low to moderate intensity for a long duration. After 90 seconds, the aerobic energy system starts to work and begins making energy. This can be used by an athlete as their glycolysis energy system is winding down to help them to continue at a moderate level of intensity.

Knowledge recap

1. What is meant by aerobic?
2. Where do we get fatty acids?

Assessment guidance for learning aim B

Scenario

You have secured a voluntary work placement with a sports coaching company. The manager has asked you to help some of the young athletes (aged 13 to 14 years) who attend coaching sessions. The young athletes often struggle to understand the energy systems which their bodies need to fuel their different events. To assist the athletes, the manager has asked you to produce a presentation to help them to learn about energy systems. You will also need to show how the energy systems are used in different sporting situations.

2B.P5 Describe the function of the three energy systems in the production and release of energy for sports performance

Assessor report: The command verb in the grading criterion is describe. In learners' answers we would expect to see a detailed account of the three energy systems in the production and release of energy for sports performance.

Learner answer

ATP

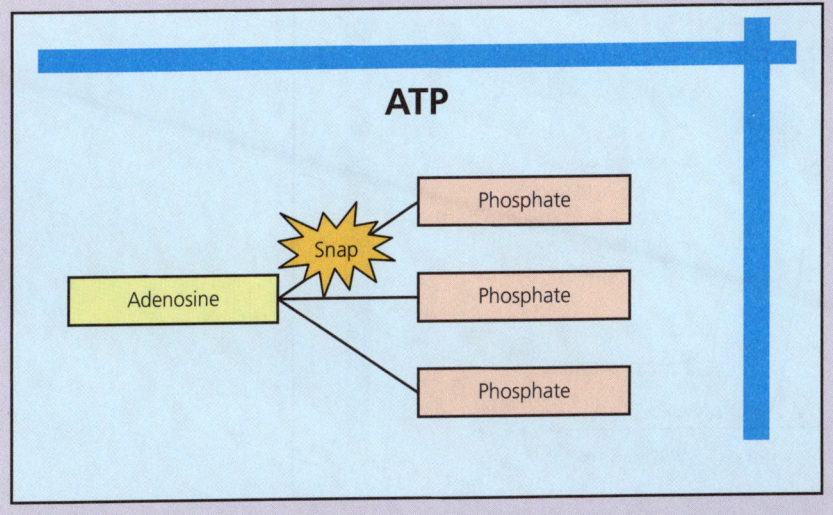

Main energy pathways

ATP-CP – Immediate energy supply
(4–20 seconds)

Lactic acid – Intermediate energy supply
(20–240 seconds)

Aerobic – Long-term energy supply
(240–600 seconds)

The function of the aerobic energy system

- To produce energy after 240 and for up to 600 seconds.
- To convert glucose and oxygen into energy, carbon dioxide and water.
- To produce energy by using oxygen.
- When the body has run out of glucose the body can use fatty acids as a fuel source.
- Sports using this energy system are low intensity and high duration, for example long-distance running, a marathon or a triathlon.
- This energy system can keep going as long as it has a fuel source, glucose or fatty acids.

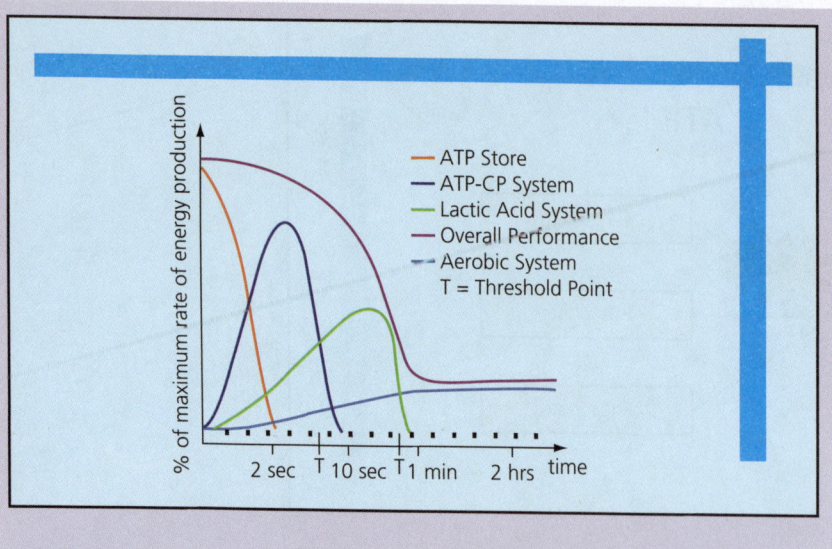

Which energy system is used?

It depends on these:

- The type of activity or sport
- The speed of the task
- The intensity of the task
- Duration of the task

Assessor report: The candidate has described the function of the aerobic energy system. To achieve the criterion for 2B.P5, they need to describe the functions of the other two energy systems and release of energy for sports performance.

Assessor report – overall

What is good about this assessment evidence?

The learner has produced six PowerPoint slides. They have mentioned the three different energy systems and have included a diagram to show how the energy systems overlap. The learner has made some effort to describe when each energy system will be dominant. The learner has produced a good template from which the work could be developed to achieve 2B.P5 by adding descriptions of the lactic acid and ATP-CP energy systems.

What could be improved in this assessment evidence?

The learner has not produced enough evidence to meet the criterion for 2B.P5. They should include more slides to show their understanding of the energy systems, or they could add notes to their existing slides. The learner needs to ensure that they have described the function of all three energy systems; they must describe how these energy systems can fuel sports performance. The learner could focus on one sport for each energy system and describe its function in energy release, or they could look at one sport and identify the different activities in that sport which use the three different energy systems.

2B.M5 Using two selected sports, explain how the body uses both the anaerobic and aerobic energy systems

Assessor report: The command verb in the grading criterion is explain. In their answers we would expect to see that the learner had developed the points made for the pass criteria, and had provided more depth on how the body uses both the anaerobic and aerobic energy systems for two selected sports.

Learner answer

How the body uses anaerobic and aerobic energy systems in boxing and tennis

ATP

ATP is the body's power source. ATP is made up of an adenosine molecule and 3 phosphates. Every time the bonds between the adenosine and the phosphates break energy is released. Our body uses that energy to fuel our body, whether this is sprinting in athletics or itching our nose.
ATP provides the energy for our body to move.

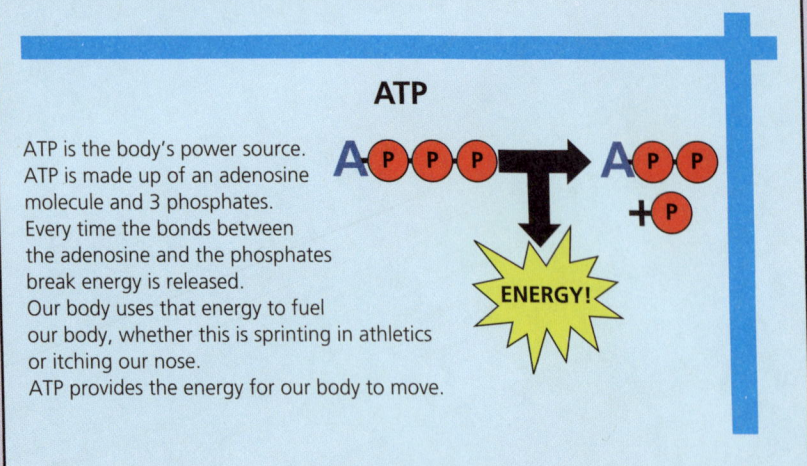

Energy systems

Anaerobic energy systems
ATP-CP (4–20 seconds)
Lactic acid (20–240 seconds)
Aerobic energy systems
(240–600 seconds)

The **anaerobic** energy system works without using oxygen.
It provides energy for high intensity and short duration activities.
The **aerobic** energy system uses oxygen to produce energy.
It provides energy for low intensity and long duration activities.

Boxing

Boxing is a sport which involves a lot of power, muscular endurance, speed and strength.

Boxers have to be able to deliver blow after blow, dodge and defend.

Boxing matches last for 12 rounds of 3 minutes.

Which energy system does a boxer use?

- The punch a boxer delivers is very quick, less than a second and it has to be very powerful. The energy system which fuels this jab is the anaerobic ATP-CP system.
- When the boxer is ducking and dodging around the ring he is using the anaerobic lactic acid system which gives him high intensity energy for the duration of each round.
- For the duration of the bout the boxer is having to defend and attack, moving around he is being fuelled by the aerobic energy system. This gives him the energy to keep going throughout the 12 rounds if he needs to.

Tennis

Tennis is a sport which involves a lot of muscular endurance, flexibility, speed and strength.

Tennis players have to be able to produce powerful serves, return slow net shots and smash overhead backline drives.

Men's tennis matches can last for over five hours!

Which energy systems does a tennis player use?

- To give the tennis player the high intensity energy he needs to serve he uses the ATP-CP anaerobic energy system. This gives him the power to deliver a short strong serve.
- When the tennis players are playing for a point they are either serving or receiving, the player needs to sprint around the court making sure that he is in the right position to return the ball. The energy system used to fuel this high intensity short duration activity will be the anaerobic lactic acid system.
- To allow the tennis player to last the duration of a five hour tennis match the player uses the aerobic energy system. This provides him with long duration, low intensity energy.

Summary

- The sports person's body will be trained to know which energy system to use, when and why.

- The choice of energy system depends on the duration and intensity of the activity.

- Energy systems will overlap, with more than one providing energy at any time.

- I have focused on the dominant energy source in my discussions.

Assessor report: The learner has selected tennis and boxing to explain how the body uses both the anaerobic and aerobic energy systems. The learner has produced annotated PowerPoint slides as evidence for this criterion.

Assessor report – overall

What is good about this assessment evidence?

The learner has provided eight PowerPoint slides. Most of the slides include some annotations. The learner has chosen two suitable sports, boxing and tennis. The learner has shown some good understanding of the topic by applying their knowledge to the different sports situations when each energy system becomes dominant. The learner has identified sports activities which use the anaerobic and aerobic energy systems. The learner has presented their work well.

What could be improved in this assessment evidence?

To achieve 2B.M5 the learner needs to include more detail about how the different energy systems fuel different sports activities. The learner has not given any real background on the energy systems. They should include the methods utilised by the energy systems and the fuel sources they require. The learner has made some attempt to state how and why each energy system becomes dominant, but this lacks real depth. To help the learner to achieve the 2B.M5 criterion, it may be useful for the learner to include notes pages with each slide. This provides them with more room to expand on their explanations of each slide.

2B.D2 Compare and contrast how the energy systems are used in sports with different demands

Assessor report: The command verbs in the grading criterion are *compare* and *contrast*. In the answer we would expect to see that the learner had identified the main factors in two or more situations, and then explained the similarities and differences of how the energy systems are used in sports with different demands.

✎ Learner answer

How energy systems are used in sports with different demands

Anaerobic and aerobic energy systems

High demand for energy – Anaerobic
Explosive activities
E.g. Javelin throw, high jump, golf swing

Medium demand for energy – Anaerobic
Short bursts of energy
E.g. 1500 m, 200 m swim

Low demand for energy – Aerobic
Sustained activity
E.g. Long-distance events, marathons

Slide 2 notes

Sports activities which have a high demand for energy (explosive activities such as a javelin throw, high jump or golf swing) will use the ATP-CP anaerobic energy system. These activities demand high amounts of energy but only for a short period of time. These activities are not repeated; they tend to be a one-off movement. This includes a throw, a kick or something that needs a big amount of energy immediately!

Sports which have a medium demand for energy tend to have activities with short bursts of energy, such as a 1500 m run or 200 m swim. These activities need energy to keep the athlete going for more than just a one-off movement, but they still require high intensity energy. They are almost the intensity of a sprint, but need to keep going to complete their activity. These types of activity are fuelled by the anaerobic lactic acid system.

Activities with a low demand for energy, which need the energy sustained for the duration of the event or match (such as long-distance events like a marathon or an open water swim), need low intensity energy for a long duration. These long duration, low intensity activities will use the aerobic energy system to provide energy for their event.

Energy systems

Anaerobic energy systems
ATP-CP (4–20 seconds) and lactic acid (20–240 seconds)

Aerobic energy system
(240–600 seconds)

The anaerobic energy system works without using oxygen. It provides energy for high intensity and short duration activities.

The aerobic energy system uses oxygen to produce energy. It provides energy for low intensity and long duration activities.

Slide 3 notes

The **ATP-CP energy system** produces ATP very quickly. It is used for events such as the high jump or long jump. It makes energy without oxygen; it is an anaerobic energy system. This energy system can provide energy for four to twenty seconds. To make energy, the CP bond breaks into creatine and phosphate, and this bond-breaking releases energy. Later, during recovery, the aerobic energy system is used to join the creatine and phosphate back together. There is only a small amount of CP in our bodies, so when this runs out, the glycolysis/lactic acid anaerobic energy system starts up.

The **glycolysis or lactic acid anaerobic system** makes energy quite quickly. It is used for events such as the 800 m run or 100 m swim. These types of event are moderate to high intensity and will last 20–45 seconds. This energy system produces a waste product called lactic acid.

This energy system is also anaerobic; it makes energy without using oxygen. After 45 seconds and up to 240 seconds, this energy system uses glycogen stored in the muscles. As the system begins to stop working as effectively (at around 240 seconds), the aerobic energy system takes over.

The **aerobic energy system** makes energy at a much slower rate than the two anaerobic systems. It makes energy for long-duration events, such as a marathon or a triathlon, when the exercise is at a lower intensity. This energy system uses oxygen, which is why it is called the aerobic energy system. This system uses glycogen stored in the muscles and fatty acids to make energy.

Assessor report: The learner has produced only three PowerPoint slides in which they have attempted to compare and contrast how the energy systems are used in sports with different demands. To meet the 2B.D2 criterion, the learner needs to complete this piece of work; the whole set of slides and notes needs to be included.

Assessor report – overall

What is good about this assessment evidence?

The learner has produced some good evidence and has begun to compare and contrast the different energy systems. The learner has provided sports examples for each energy system and has stated why these are suited. The learner has included notes with their PowerPoint slides. The learner has applied themselves at the correct level for 2B.D2 but they have not completed the piece of work.

What could be improved in this assessment evidence?

To achieve the 2B.D2 criterion, the learner needs to compare and contrast how the energy systems are used in sports with different demands. The learner has attempted this criterion and has produced three PowerPoint slides with notes. To achieve the criterion, the work needs to be completed. The learner must explain how the energy systems differ, what they need to work most efficiently, and what (if any) waste products they make. The learner should go into much more detail about each energy system, identify what is good and bad about each system and state which sports are fuelled by the systems and why. The learner could also look at how sports performers can adapt their bodies to utilise specific energy systems. For example, does training in an anaerobic zone increase the performer's ability to cope with lactic acid? Will this help performance?

Sample assignment brief: Learning aim A

Assignment title	Responding and adapting to exercise
Learning aim	2A
Criteria covered	2A.P1, 2A.P2, 2A.P3, 2A.P4, 2A.M1, 2A.M2, 2A.M3, 2A.M4, 2A.D1
Assessment evidence	Leaflets, posters, or individual or small-group PowerPoint presentations

Scenario

Your school has just had a new gym built next to the sports hall. The gym manager has asked your BTEC Sport group to create an information pack to show how the body adapts to exercise. This information will be displayed in your school gym so that other learners can see the benefits of taking part in exercise.

Task 1

Musculoskeletal system responses to short-term exercise

Produce information about the musculoskeletal system responses to exercise.

You will need to show how the musculoskeletal system changes as it responds to exercise, using sports examples and scenarios.

You might include information about how these responses can affect performance.

This task should be presented as an information leaflet.

Task 2

Cardiorespiratory system responses to short-term exercise

Produce information about the cardiorespiratory system responses to exercise.

You will need to show how the cardiorespiratory system changes as it responds to exercise, using sports examples and scenarios.

You might include information about how these responses can affect performance.

This task should be presented as a table which can be added to your leaflet from Task 1.

Task 3

Long-term adaptations of the musculoskeletal system to exercise

Produce information about the long-term adaptations of the musculoskeletal system to exercise.

You will need to show how the musculoskeletal system changes as it responds to long-term exercise, using different sports examples and scenarios.

You might include information about how these responses can increase performance.

This task should be presented as a set of posters.

Task 4

Long-term adaptations of the cardiorespiratory system to exercise

Produce information about the long-term adaptations of the cardiorespiratory system to exercise.

You will need to show how the cardiorespiratory system changes as it responds to long-term exercise, using different sports examples and scenarios.

You might include information about how these responses can increase performance.

This task should be presented as a set of posters.

Task 5

How the musculoskeletal and cardiorespiratory systems respond and adapt to exercise

Produce information about the long-term adaptations of the musculoskeletal and cardiorespiratory system to exercise.

You will need to show how the musculoskeletal and cardiorespiratory systems change as they respond to long-term exercise, using different sports examples and scenarios.

You might include information about how these responses can increase performance.

This task should be presented as an annotated poster.

Sample assignment brief: Learning aim B

Assignment title	Energy for sports performance
Learning aim	2B
Criteria covered	2B.P5, 2B.M5, 2B.D2
Assessment evidence	PowerPoint presentation

Scenario

You have secured a voluntary work placement with a sports coaching company. The manager has asked you to help some of the young athletes (aged 13 to 14 years) who attend coaching sessions. The young athletes often struggle to understand the energy systems which they need to fuel their different events. To assist the athletes, the manager has asked you to produce a presentation to help them to learn about energy systems. You will also need to show how the energy systems are used in different sporting situations.

Task 1

The function of energy systems

Produce information about the different energy systems. You will need to show how the energy systems are used in different sporting situations, and give sports examples for each system.

You might include how the energy systems use changes during sports activities, and how sports people can use energy systems to their advantage to benefit their sports performance.

This task should be presented as a PowerPoint presentation. You can work as an individual or in groups of two or three.

Knowledge recap answers

Topic A.1, page 4
1. The fluid which surrounds a synovial joint, acting as a lubricant to allow the joint to move easily.
2. An increase in muscle temperature; an increase in the range of movement at joints.
3. Chemical processes/reactions occurring within your body that make energy.

Topic A.2, page 8
1. The number of heart beats per minute.
2. Narrowing of the arterioles.
3. A waste product made when the body uses glucose without oxygen to make energy.
4. During exercise, blood pressure increases. The systolic pressure rises and the diastolic pressure remains the same.
5. The amount of air inhaled and exhaled with each breath.

Topic A.3, page 13
1. An increase in the size of muscle tissue.
2. Ligaments hold bone to bone, while tendons connect bone to muscle.
3. Small structures inside our muscle cells which produce energy in the form of ATP.
4. Regular exercise will make our bones stronger and denser. This will help to prevent the bones losing calcium and weakening.

Topic A.4, page 17
1. Cardiac hypertrophy occurs when the heart has grown larger and stronger.
2. Anywhere between 50 and 70 ml.
3. If the resting heart rate is lower than 60 bpm, the heart is working more efficiently. This means that an athlete can cope much better working at higher intensities; their heart rate can go higher without the athlete fatiguing.
4. Carbon dioxide and water.

Topics B.1 and B.2, page 39
1. Without oxygen.
2. A golf swing and an uppercut in boxing.
3. A molecule in our muscle cells which produces energy.
4. Four to twenty seconds.
5. The breakdown of glucose to produce energy.

Topic B.3, page 41
1. A type of glucose which is stored in the muscle cells and the liver.
2. A waste product, created when glucose is broken down to make energy without using oxygen.
3. Waste products are harmful to the body and can cause fatigue.

Topic B.4, page 43
1. Using oxygen.
2. Fatty acids are found in oils, nuts, seeds and oily fish.